Mysterious Encounters

Curses

by Rachel Lynette

KIDHAVEN PRESS
A part of Gale, Cengage Learning

GALE
CENGAGE Learning

Detroit • New York • San Francisco • New Haven, Conn • Waterville, Maine • London

LIBRARY OF CONGRESS CATALOGING-IN-PUBLICATION DATA

Lynette, Rachel.
  Curses / by Rachel Lynette.
      p. cm. -- (Mysterious encounters)
  Includes bibliographical references and index.
  ISBN 978-0-7377-5422-3 (hardcover)
  1. Blessing and cursing--Juvenile literature. 2. Occultism--Juvenile literature. I. Title.
  BF1558.L96 2011
  398'.41--dc22

                                                                    2010043803

KidHaven Press
27500 Drake Rd.
Farmington Hills, MI 48331

ISBN-13: 978-0-7377-5422-3
ISBN-10: 0-7377-5422-2

Printed in the United States of America
1 2 3 4 5 6 7 14 13 12 11 10

Printed by Bang Printing, Brainerd, MN, 1st Ptg., 01/2011

Contents

Chapter 1

Cursed!

Until 1945 the Chicago Cubs were a winning baseball team. They had won two World Series and sixteen division titles, called pennants. On October 6, 1945, the Cubs were playing in the World Series when a man named Billy Sianis decided to take his pet goat Murphy to the fourth game. Sianis was hoping the goat would bring the Cubs luck, but the goat's bad smell caused Sianis and Murphy to be kicked out of Chicago's Wrigley Field. As the pair was leaving, an angry Sianis yelled, "Them Cubs, they aren't gonna win no more!"[1] The Cubs, indeed, lost that game and went on to lose the World Series, too. So began the Curse of the Billy Goat, which has continued for more than 65 years.

Since 1945, the Cubs have not won a single pennant or played in even one World Series game.

What Is a Curse?

The Curse of the Billy Goat is just one of many famous curses. Most famous curses involve people who are already in the spotlight, such as sports teams, movie stars, and political figures. However, there are plenty of curses that affect people who are not famous.

A curse usually starts when one person wishes harm to another person or group of people. The curse may be written or spoken. Sometimes the person performing the curse calls on **supernatural** powers, such as God or even the devil, to help make the curse happen. A curse also may be used to protect something, such as a tomb or treasure.

Voodoo priests hold a voodoo doll, which can represent a person that someone wants to curse.

Anyone can make a curse, but many people believe that the curse will not work unless it comes from a person who can tap into supernatural powers. This may be a priest, a person who believes in **voodoo**, or someone who claims to be a witch. Often people who perform curses have special rituals, such as the chanting of spells or the use of a human-shaped figure to represent the person being cursed.

Not all curses are focused on specific people. Sometimes an object or place might be cursed. People who come into contact with that cursed object may encounter misfortune or even death. People who visit cursed places might also find themselves in danger. In some cases, a curse is not known to be started by a particular person. It surfaces after a series of bad luck occurs.

The Power of Belief

Some curses may work not because of any supernatural power, but simply because the victim believes in the curse. For instance, if a man knows that a powerful voodoo curse has been put on him, he may become so frightened that he has a heart attack and dies.

Curses, Jinxes, and Hexes

A curse is similar to a jinx or hex, but there are some small differences among them. A hex is a spell or bewitchment aimed at a specific person. Although most people think of a hex as something that is meant to cause harm, a hex can be used for good purposes, too. Hexes are commonly associated with witches.

A jinx is a cause of constant bad luck. Often an object is thought to be jinxed when it seems to

A witch uses different symbolic items to cast a hex.

bring misfortune to the bearer. Usually, a jinx is less severe than a hex or a curse. For example, a person carrying a jinxed umbrella while walking to a bus stop is likely to miss the bus, whereas a person carrying a hexed umbrella is likely to be run over by the bus.

A curse is more like a hex than a jinx, but unlike a hex, a curse is never a good thing for the person being cursed. A curse is always meant to bring misfortune.

Are Curses Real?

No one can prove whether a curse can be the true source of bad luck. A person who has been cursed and dies shortly afterward may have died anyway, with or without the curse. Certainly, there are many cases in which curses have not worked. People curse others all the time. For example, a person who wishes out loud for another person to drop dead—whether in anger or not—is, in a way, creating a curse. In most cases, the person doing the cursing does not really mean what is said and, fortunately, the cursed person rarely does drop dead. Even if a person is sincere and truly does want to cause harm to another person, there is no scientific proof that cursing the person will actually cause the victim harm.

However, there are cases when events seem to prove that a curse really is effective. The Billy Goat curse is one such case. The Cubs' losing streak cer-

Sam Sianis, nephew of Billy Sianis, the man who is said to have put a curse on the Chicago Cubs in 1945, has taken his goat to Wrigley Field in an attempt to end the team's stretch of disappointing playoff results.

tainly is unusual, and it did start as soon as Sianis made his curse. On the other hand, the Cubs' losing record after that fateful day in 1945 could be pure coincidence. There is no scientific proof to determine if the Cubs' losing streak has been the result of Sianis's curse or simply a very long run of bad luck.

Lifting a Curse

Curses that are directed at a specific person may end when that person dies—either from events related to the curse or from natural causes. However, some curses go on for years and years and are difficult to reverse.

Do Not Blame the Witch

Women who practice the Wiccan religion call themselves witches and claim they can do magic. Although these modern-day witches have been accused of casting evil spells and cursing other people, they are unlikely to harm anyone. Wiccans believe that if they curse another person, the curse will come back to them three times as strong.

Several attempts were made to break the Billy Goat curse. For instance, the Cubs tried to reverse the curse in 1984 by bringing a billy goat back into Wrigley Field. By that time Billy Sianis had died, so his nephew Sam was invited to the stadium with a goat. Sam Sianis and the goat were escorted to the center of the field. Then Sianis raised his hands and declared that the curse was lifted. At first, the attempt seemed to work: The Cubs won game after game. But by the end of the season, the team still had not made it to the World Series. Other tries to lift the curse followed the same pattern: A promising start to the season was followed by a disappointing finish. This is one curse that refuses to go away.

Chapter 2

Historical Curses

Belief in curses was much more common in the past than it is today. People were more superstitious years ago, because they did not understand things about the world that science has later explained. For example, hundreds of years ago when someone suddenly got sick and died, that person was sometimes suspected of being cursed, perhaps by an angry neighbor. Today the causes of many diseases are widely known, so people do not assume that illnesses are brought on by curses. In the past, however, curses were blamed not just for deaths but for misfortunes of all kinds, including earthquakes and failing crops.

Bibical Curses

Not all curses come from humans. The Old Testament of the Bible contains many curses from God. One of God's curses appears in the first book of the Bible, called Genesis. It is a **vengeance** curse. In the story, God curses Cain for killing his brother, Abel. He says, "Now you are under a curse and driven from the ground which opened its mouth to receive your brother's blood from your hand. When you work the ground, it will no longer yield its crops for you. You will be a restless wanderer on earth."[2]

This image depicts God descending to put a curse on Cain after he killed his brother, Abel.

In the Bible's book of Deuteronomy (doo-tuh-RON-uh-me), God threatens to rain down curses on anyone who does not obey him. These curses include disease; madness; blindness; defeat by enemies; loss of land, animals, and children; and having one's **carcass** eaten by birds.

There are fewer curses in the Bible's New Testament. In the book of Mark, Jesus approaches a fig tree in hopes of finding figs to eat, but it is not the season for figs. He curses the tree and it withers and dies. Later, after Jesus's death, the apostle Paul curses all people who do not love the Lord. However, Paul's curse is not specific. He does not say what misfortunes will happen to those whom he has cursed. Although people in biblical times took curses quite seriously, today most people do not believe that a curse can really cause bad events to occur.

Ancient Greek and Roman Binding Curses

In the times of ancient Greece and Rome, most people believed in the supernatural. The Greek and Roman religions were rich in myths that featured powerful gods, frightening monsters, and mythical places. Ancient Greeks and Romans also believed that they could call upon specific gods and goddesses to help a curse. Hades (HAY-dees), Hecate (HEH-cuh-tee), Persephone (per-SEH-fuh-nee),

Lost Curse Tablets

Archaeologists know that in addition to lead, curses also were written on wax, papyrus, and clay. However, few of these tablets have survived because unlike lead, the other materials can break apart underground. For this reason many tablets have been lost forever.

and Hermes (HER-mees) were frequently called upon because they are the gods most closely associated with the dead and the underworld, the place where the dead go.

Many curses were written on tablets. A curse tablet was usually made from a thin sheet of lead that was about the size of a playing card. Tablets could also be made from wax, **papyrus** (puh-PIE-russ), or clay. In addition to the written curse, the tablet might have contained symbols or pictures, too. Upon finishing the curse, the creator would roll up the tablet and drive a nail through it. It was thought that the nail would bring even more pain to the victim of the curse. In order to give the curse the power to work, the tablet was buried. The curse was most effective if the tablet was buried in a graveyard or close to where the victim lived or worked. Wells

A cursing stone from 16th century Britain was carved with a curse against Scottish raiders. The ancient Greeks and Romans also wrote curses on stones and tablets.

where the victim drew water were also popular burial spots. Sometimes the tablet was buried with an object that the cursed person owned or strands of hair from that person's head. Figures made from clay or wax that represented the cursed person were sometimes buried with the tablet.

Many of the curses were meant to make the victim perform poorly during a legal trial. These are called binding spells. Binding spells were also used to make an actor, musician, or athlete perform badly. The following binding spell was found in a grave. In it, the author is asking demons to bind a **chariot** driver. It reads,

> Bind every limb and every sinew [tendon] of Victoricus, the charioteer of the Blue team

... and of the horses he is about to race. ... Bind their legs, their onrush, their bounding, their running, blind their eyes so they cannot see and twist their soul and heart so that they cannot breathe. Just as this rooster has been bound by its feet, hands and head, so bind the legs and hands and head and heart of Victoricus, the charioteer of the Blue team, for tomorrow.[3]

Over 1,500 lead curse tablets have been found. Most were found in Greece, but some were discovered in Great Britain. The oldest of the tablets dates back to the late 6th century B.C. Most of the curses are written by and about common people rather than the wealthy and the powerful. The tablets are one reason why **archaeologists** (are-kee-AHL-uh-jists) believe that curses and other forms of magic were an accepted part of everyday life in ancient Greece and Rome.

Curses in the Middle Ages

Hundreds of years later, people still believed in magic. However, with the rise of Christianity in Europe, a major change occurred. In ancient Greece, magic was not only a common part of life, but also legal and accepted by the people. Christianity took the opposite view. Early Christians believed that magic was from the devil and those who performed magic were the devil's servants—evil witches who

A drawing depicts a woman thought to be a witch being burned. Witch hunts in Europe and the English colonies led to the deaths of many people.

had sold their souls to the devil. When something bad happened, such as the death of a child, people blamed it on a witch's curse. Usually, the people being accused of performing witchcraft were women who were poor, unmarried, and generally disliked by the community.

One such woman was Isobel Shyrie, who lived in the town of Forfar, Scotland. Shyrie was poor and could not pay her taxes. In 1661 she got into an argument with a tax collector named Baillie George Wood. During the argument, she cursed Wood, who suddenly dropped dead. Shyrie was immediately accused of witchcraft and taken to the town dungeon. Soon after, her friends were also arrested. The youngest was a girl of thirteen who was thought to be a witch simply because her mother was accused of being one. The accused women were tortured until they gave the names of other "witches" and confessed to many acts of witchcraft. Some women died in the dungeon. Others were publicly executed by being strangled and then burned in the center of the town. When the witch hunt finally ended, 22 women had been killed.

Voodoo Curses

The Middle Ages was a long time ago, but curses have been blamed for deaths in the not so distant past as well. Voodoo is a religion with African roots that came to the United States with the slaves. It was especially popular in New Orleans, Louisiana. People who practice voodoo claim that they can do several kinds of magic, including communicating with the dead and putting curses on people. Residents of New Orleans might find black candles, miniature coffins, and voodoo dolls near their front doors letting them know they have been cursed. Many would seek protection from these curses, usually in the form of small bags of herbs or animal remains called gris-gris (GREE-gree) bags or other good luck charms. Maybe if New Orleans resident Rosita Zerruda had had such a charm, she would have met a kinder fate.

The police were called to Zerruda's house on November 2, 1950, when the neighbors heard children screaming. They found Zerruda with a can of kerosene, trying to burn down her house. She had deep gashes on her arm that she had

Voodoo dolls for sale in a market in New Orleans. The dolls are thought to put curses on people.

clearly made herself. The police followed a trail of blood to a bedroom where they found Zerruda's four children, who also had gashes on their arms. The family was rushed to the hospital where their wounds were treated. However, when questioned by the police, Zerruda claimed that her neighbor, who practiced voodoo, had cursed her. She said she had found blood and a black wreath on her doorstep that morning. That was all the information the police could get, because before they could question Zerruda further, she started to stutter and twitch, then suddenly fell into a coma. She never recovered.

The Curse of King Tut

Sometimes, an ancient curse can find its way to modern times. Or at least that is what many people thought happened in Egypt when archaeologist Howard Carter and his team opened the tomb of King Tutankhamen (too-tahn-KAH-men), also known as King Tut, on November 26, 1922. The treasures they found were astounding, but soon after strange events started to occur. There were rumors that the archaeologists had also found a mummy's curse in the tomb.

First, the man who had paid to have the tomb dug up, Lord Carnarvon, died less than a year after the tomb was opened. He had gotten sick after being bitten by a mosquito. After that, the rumors

Archaeologist Howard Carter and an assistant examine the remains of King Tutankhamen. Carter and others who opened King Tut's tomb are said to have experienced the mummy's curse.

Mummy Mold

Rather than a mummy's curse, it is likely that ancient mold found in King Tut's tomb was the real killer of Lord Carnarvon, the man who paid to have the tomb opened. He died just a few months later. Mold enters the body through the nose or the mouth and can cause organ failure and death, especially in people who are already weak or sick.

started. A reporter said that Carter had found a tablet in the tomb with the words "Death will slay with his wings whoever disturbs the peace of the pharaoh."[4] Although Carter denied the existence of the tablet, which was never found, more rumors followed. It was said that Carnarvon's dog, thousands of miles away in England, dropped dead at the same time as his master, and that all the lights went out in Cairo, Egypt, at the very moment of his death. Over the next fifteen years, 21 people who had been associated with the tomb died. With each death, belief in the mummy's curse increased.

In recent years many of the claims about the curse have been proven false, but the curse lives on as people continue to wonder if King Tut really did take revenge on those who **desecrated** his tomb.

Chapter 3

In the Spotlight

Many well-known curses focus on famous people. Famous people are already in the spotlight—they constantly are followed by photographers and bothered for interviews—so, whatever they do or say becomes a topic for the general public to discuss. In this way, relatively small events can become bigger when they happen to a celebrity. In addition, rumors, whether true or not, can add to a story, making it more exciting than it really is. Therefore, an offhand remark could be considered a curse, at least in the eyes of the public.

The Curse of the Bambino

As one of the greatest players in baseball, George

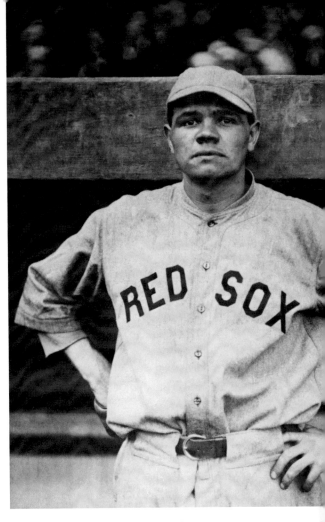

Baseball legend Babe Ruth spent his early career with the Boston Red Sox. His trade to the New York Yankees in 1920 is said to have put a curse on the Red Sox team.

Herman "Babe" Ruth, who was known as the Bambino, was famous for his many homeruns and his likable personality. However, he also is associated with a curse that lasted 86 years! The curse's victims were the Boston Red Sox. Before the curse the Red Sox were a popular and successful baseball team. In fact, the Red Sox won the very first World Series, in 1903, and won four more Series by 1918.

Babe Ruth played for the Red Sox from 1914 until 1919, when he was traded to the New York Yankees. The Yankees had never made it to the World Series until Ruth joined the team. After that, the Yankees won the World Series year after year.

Altogether, the Yankees won 26 World Series between 1919 and 2004, twice as many as any other team. The Red Sox, on the other hand, went into a slump after trading away Ruth. They did not even make it to the World Series again until 1946, and they lost that Series four games to three. After that, they reached the World Series only four more times and lost each time. It was not until 2004, 56 years after the Bambino's death, that the Sox won the World Series again and broke the 86-year curse at last.

The Forever 27 Club

The death of a national idol is always a tragedy, but there has been a somewhat disturbing trend with musicians: Many of them have died at the age of 27. This trend, labeled the "Forever 27 Club," makes some people believe that a curse may be to blame.

The first well-known musician to die at age 27 was Brian Jones. Jones had played guitar for the British rock band the Rolling Stones. He drowned in a swimming pool while **intoxicated** in 1969. A year later, two more musicians joined the Forever 27 Club: guitar legend Jimi Hendrix, who died from choking following an overdose of sleeping pills, and singer Janis Joplin, who died of a **heroin** overdose. The lead singer of the Doors, Jim Morrison, joined the club when he died in 1971. These four musicians were all rock icons. They all knew each other and all died within a two-year period.

More recently, Kurt Cobain, lead singer of the rock band Nirvana, became a member of the club when he committed suicide in 1994.

In addition to these superstars, over 40 lesser-known musicians also died at age 27. Author Charles R. Cross has written biographies on both Hendrix and Cobain. He says, "The number of musicians who passed away at 27 is truly remarkable by any standard. Though humans die regularly at all ages, there is a statistical spike for musicians who die at 27."[5]

Nirvana singer Kurt Cobain committed suicide in 1994 when he was 27 years old, the same age at which several other music legends also died.

Joining the Club Intentionally?

After musician and singer Kurt Cobain committed suicide in 1994, some people said that he may have killed himself at age 27 in order to join the Forever 27 Club. This is unlikely, however, because Cobain had a long history of depression and drug addiction and had already tried to kill himself several times during his life.

Movie Curses

Many frightening events occur in horror movies, but bad things do not usually happen to the actors and other crew members in real life. Unfortunately, this is not always the case. Several horror movies are thought to be cursed because of the tragic deaths associated with them.

Director Roman Polanski's 1968 movie *Rosemary's Baby* is about a woman who gives birth to the son of Satan (the devil). A year after the movie was released, Polanski's wife was murdered while she was eight months pregnant. In that same year the film's producer, William Castle, was hospitalized for kidney failure. During his recovery he

Actress Heather O'Rourke is one of four people associated with the Poltergeist movies who met a sudden and unexpected death. Many people wondered if a curse was to blame.

learned that Krzysztof Komeda, the composer who wrote the music for the film, was also in the same hospital. The composer died of a blood clot within a month—in a similar way as one of the characters in the movie.

The first *Poltergeist* movie was released in 1982. Two more followed in 1986 and 1988. The movies are about a family who moves into a house that is haunted by trouble-making, restless spirits. Eerily, four deaths were associated with the *Poltergeist* films. The first death occurred November 4, 1982, just a few months after the release of the original film. Twenty-two-year-old actress Dominique Dunne, who played the oldest child in the family, was strangled to death by her ex-boyfriend. The next two to die were both in *Poltergeist II*. In 1985, 60-year-old Julian Beck died of stomach cancer, and in 1987 53-year-old Will Sampson died of complications from an organ transplant. The final death, on February 1, 1988, was perhaps the most heartbreaking. Twelve-year-old Heather O'Rourke, who had played the youngest child in all three movies, died suddenly of septic shock. Her unexpected death shocked and saddened her family, friends, and fans. O'Rourke was buried in the same cemetery as Dunne.

The Superman Curse

Everyone knows about Superman, the indestructible "Man of Steel," but many people do not know about the Superman curse. Over the years since Superman was created in the 1930s by DC Comics, various writers, actors, directors, and others associated with the character have suffered misfortunes ranging from bankruptcy to death. The most famous of these tragedies happened to two actors with similar names who both had played Superman: George Reeves and Christopher Reeve.

George Reeves portrayed Superman in the television series *The Adventures of Superman*, which ran from 1951 to 1958. On June 16, 1959, just days before he was to be married, Reeves was found shot in his bedroom. Although the death was ruled a suicide, many people believed the actor had ac-

Superman actor Christopher Reeve is one of several people associated with the character who experienced tragedy, said to be the result of a curse.

tually been murdered. Friends and family claimed that he was not the kind of person who would commit suicide and that he was not unhappy. The case remains a mystery to this day.

Years later actor Christopher Reeve played Superman and Clark Kent in the 1978 movie version of *Superman*. The movie was a huge hit and was followed by three more Superman films starring Reeve. With his stunning good looks, Reeve rose to stardom and had no problem getting other roles.

Everything changed in May 1995, however, when Reeve was thrown from a horse during a riding competition. Reeve's spinal cord was broken and he was **paralyzed** from the neck down. In 2004 Reeve died from a heart attack that was brought on by his condition. Reeve was 52 years old. Sadly, his wife, Dana, who had lovingly supported Reeve during the nine years that he was paralyzed, followed him to the grave just two years later. She died of lung cancer on March 6, 2006, at the age of 44.

Chapter 4

Cursed Places and Objects

Sometimes, it is not a person that is cursed, but rather an object or a place. When an object is cursed, misfortune seems to follow anyone who is associated with it. Cursed places bring tragedy to those who visit the area.

James Dean's Car

The Porsche 550 Spyder is a rare, fast, and shiny sports car that was made for racing. Only 90 of them were ever built, and one of them belonged to movie star James Dean. Although Dean was thrilled with his new fast car, his friends were cautious about it. When he showed it to fellow actor Alec Guinness on September 23, 1955, Guinness

The wreckage of James Dean's Porsche Spyder. The accident killed the 24-year-old actor in 1955.

warned Dean, "If you get in that Porsche, you will be dead next week."[6] Guinness's prediction proved true! Dean was killed in a near head-on collision with another car on September 30.

In the following five years, many strange events surrounded the car. A famous car specialist, George Barris, bought the wrecked Porsche. While it was being loaded onto a truck, it fell on a mechanic's legs and broke them. Some of the Porsche's parts later were installed in two different racing cars that were both linked to tragedies. One of the cars crashed into a tree, killing the driver. The other car flipped over, and the driver suffered many injuries. In addition, two of the tires of the Porsche Spyder were sold to a man who installed them on another car. That car nearly crashed after both tires blew out at the same time.

Barris loaned the wrecked car to the California Highway Patrol so it could use the car to demonstrate to teenagers the importance of automobile safety. A few days later, however, the garage in which the Porsche was being stored burned down and every car in that garage, except for the Spyder, was destroyed. Mishaps and injuries continued to surround the wrecked car until 1960, when it mysteriously disappeared while being transported to Los Angeles. To this day, no one knows what happened to the infamous vehicle.

The Hope Diamond

As with James Dean's car, the Hope Diamond seems to have brought tragedy to many who have come in contact with it. The diamond's history began in India, where the 112 **carat** blue diamond was believed to represent an eye on a Hindu statue. According to legend, when the diamond was stolen, angry local priests cursed it. French jewel trader Jean-Baptiste Tavernier eventually bought the diamond for an unknown amount and took it back to Europe. Although the legend also claims that Tavernier died soon after and that his body was torn apart by wild dogs, this has been proven

A 1915 photo shows Evalyn McLean wearing a pendant made from the Hope Diamond.

The Hope Diamond was owned by many different people over the years. Of these, only a few suffered misfortune. Most of the people who owned the diamond lived normal, healthy lives and died of natural causes.

false. Tavernier did not die until he was 84 years old. Also, no one knows for sure whether the stone was taken from the idol, but the shape of the stone makes it unlikely that it was used as an eye.

Tavernier sold the diamond to King Louis XIV of France in 1668. Louis had the stone cut to enhance its brilliance. The cut reduced the stone to 67 carats. Although no harm came to the king, several others in the court, including the minister of finance, met unhappy ends. The diamond was passed down through the royal family until it came to King Louis XVI and his wife Marie Antoinette. Both the king and queen were beheaded during the French Revolution. The diamond was stolen in 1792. It disappeared for a while and after it reappeared in London, it was owned by several different merchants. By 1839 it had found its way to Philip Hope, for whom it is named. By this time, the diamond had been cut yet again and was now 44 carats. Eventually, the Hope family went bankrupt and the diamond was sold.

Evalyn McLean, who purchased the diamond in 1911, wore it nearly every day. Although she considered it a good luck charm, the diamond seemed to bring only bad luck to her. The bad luck included the death of her 9-year-old son in a car crash and the death of her 25-year-old daughter by suicide. Also, McLean's husband was declared insane and was committed to a mental institution.

In 1949 jeweler Harry Winston bought the diamond. He donated it to the Smithsonian Institution in 1958. Today the $3.5 million diamond is on display at the Smithsonian's National Museum of Natural History—behind 3 inches (7.6cm) of bulletproof glass!

A Cursed Song

Music can affect the way that people feel. Some music makes people happy, while other songs bring a feeling of sadness. The song *Gloomy Sunday*, for instance, is considered so sad that it has actually caused people to commit suicide. The music was written by Hungarian composer Reszo Seress in 1933 after his fiancée left him because of his lack of success. The lyrics are from a poem that was written by one of Seress's friends. Although the words are sad, it is the haunting melody that seems to cause feelings of despair and hopelessness. It has been linked to so many suicides that it has been called the "Hungarian suicide song."

The first strange incident happened after a man in the German city of Berlin requested a band to play the sad song at a tavern. He soon went home, complaining of a depressing song that was stuck in his head. That night, he shot himself. A week later, also in Berlin, a woman hanged herself in her home. The sheet music for *Gloomy Sunday* was found in her room. Strange and disturbing reports of suicides related to the song continued. One woman who had killed herself with gas had left a suicide note asking that the song be played at her funeral. A man jumped out a window after playing *Gloomy Sunday* on his piano. So many suicides followed that the song was banned in some areas.

Even the composer, Seress, could not escape his song's deadly influence. After writing to his ex-fiancée and asking her to come back to him, Seress was informed by the police that she had poisoned herself. A copy of the sheet music for *Gloomy Sunday* was found beside her. Finally, in 1968 Seress himself committed suicide by jumping out of a window.

The Bermuda Triangle

One of the best-known curses of all time is that of the Bermuda Triangle. The Bermuda Triangle is an area in the Atlantic Ocean surrounded by the Bermuda Islands, the island of Puerto Rico, and Miami, Florida. Mysterious and frightening events have happened to planes and boats that have passed through this area.

The legend started with the mysterious disappearance of Flight 19. On December 5, 1945, five U.S. Navy bombers began to experience equipment malfunctions. They later mysteriously disappeared within the triangle during a training mission. All fourteen of the crew members were lost. In addition, one of the rescue planes sent to look for

The Bermuda Triangle Is Busy, Not Cursed

John Reilly, a historian with the U.S. Naval Historical Foundation, claims that the Bermuda Triangle's record of disappearances and shipwrecks has more to do with location than with a curse. In a December 15, 2003, *National Geographic* article "Bermuda Triangle: Behind the Intrigue," Reilly says, "The region is highly traveled and has been a busy crossroads since the early days of European exploration. To say quite a few ships and airplanes have gone down there is like saying there are an awful lot of car accidents on the New Jersey Turnpike—surprise, surprise."

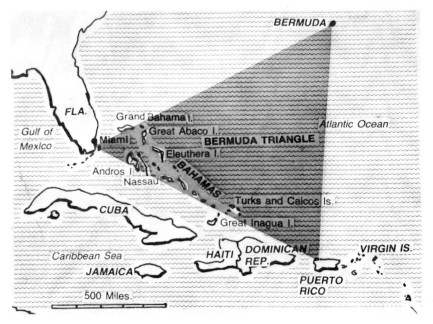

A map shows the area in the Atlantic Ocean that's known as the Bermuda Triangle, where many airplanes and ships have mysteriously crashed or disappeared.

the wreckage also disappeared, taking its thirteen-member crew with it.

Another well-known disappearance was of the SS *Marine Sulphur Queen*, a tanker ship that was carrying molten sulfur. It sank in the Bermuda Triangle in 1963. The wreckage was never found. Over 200 other incidences have been blamed on the curse of the Bermuda Triangle. These include equipment problems, sudden storms, and crashed boats and planes.

Mysterious Curses

People are fascinated by curses. The idea that a person, object, or place can be cursed is both frightening and exciting. Curses make good stories. They are full of mystery and unanswered questions. People want to know who or what caused the curse. They want to know if the victims were bad people who deserved their fates or just unlucky ones. Most of all, they want to know if the stories are true.

Jimi Hendrix, a victim of the Forever 27 Curse, made a humorous curse of his own before he died. He said, "I'm gonna put a curse on you and all your kids will be born completely naked."[7] This is one curse that will never go away!

Notes

Chapter 1

1. Quoted in Fred Bowen, "For Cubs, a Swing at the Billy Goat Curse?" *The Washington Post*, July 17, 2008. www.washingtonpost.com/wp-dyn/content/article/2008/07/16/AR2008071602638_pf.html.

Chapter 2

2. Gen. 4:11–12.
3. Quoted in Christopher A. Faraone, "When Spells Worked Magic," *Archaeological Institute of America*, 2009. www.archaeology.org/0303/etc/magic.html.
4. Quoted in Philipp Vanderberg, *The Curse of the Pharaohs*. Sevenoaks, UK: Coronet, 1975, p. 19.

Chapter 3

5. Charles R. Cross, "P-I's Writer in Residence Charles R. Cross Explores the Darker Side of 'Only the Good Die Young,'" Seattle PI, February 23, 2007. www.seattlepi.com/writers/304767_writer23.html.

Chapter 4

6. Quoted in Patrick Bernauw, "The Curse of the Little Bastard: James Dean's Porsche 550 Spyder," *A Thing for Cars*, September 2, 2009. http://athingforcars.com/autos/the-curse-of-little-bastard-james-deans-porsche-550-spyder/.
7. ThinkExist.com. http://thinkexist.com/quotes/jimi_hendrix/2.html.

Glossary

archaeologists: People who study graves, buildings, tools, and other objects to learn about cultures from the past.

carat: A unit of measurement used to determine the weight of a gem. One carat equals 200mg.

carcass: A dead body.

chariot: A two-wheeled carriage that was drawn by horses and used in ancient times for warfare and racing.

desecrated: To have damaged something that is sacred.

heroin: A dangerous, highly addictive drug that is usually injected.

intoxicated: Drunk.

papyrus: A paperlike substance that was made from a tall water plant in ancient Greece, Rome, and Egypt.

paralyzed: Unable to move.

supernatural: Relating to events that cannot be explained by natural laws in the physical world.

superstitious: Belief that is based on fear of the supernatural or luck rather than on human reason or scientific knowledge.

vengeance: Punishment for wrongdoing.

voodoo: A religious practice that involves magic and communication with the dead.

For Further Exploration

Books

David A. Kelly, *Babe Ruth and the Baseball Curse.* New York: Random House, 2009. The story of the curse and of Babe Ruth's life. Also tells how the curse was broken.

Jacqueline Morley, *King Tut's Curse!* Brighton, UK: Book House, 2007. Details the discovery of King Tut's tomb and the curse associated with it. Exciting text, full-color pictures, and a glossary.

Stephen Person, *Voodoo in New Orleans.* New York: Bearport, 2010. Tells about voodoo in the 1800s and about the Voodoo Queen, Marie Laveau. Includes full color pictures.

Karen Walker, *Mysteries of the Bermuda Triangle.* New York: Crabtree, 2008. Discusses the strange events that have occurred in the Bermuda Triangle and gives alternate explanations. Includes many pictures.

Edward Willett, *Jimi Hendrix: Kiss the Sky.* Berkeley Heights, NJ: Enslow, 2006. This biography of Jimi Hendrix includes interesting sidebars, a chronology, many quotes, and a discography of his work.

Web Sites

The Curse of Tut: Fact or Myth (www.tqnyc
.org/2002/NYC00112/index.htm). This website
provides a wealth of information not only about
the curse, but also about Howard Carter, King
Tut, the tomb, and the many treasures that were
found within it.

How the Bermuda Triangle Works, *How Stuff
Works* (http://adventure.howstuffworks.com/
bermuda-triangle.htm). This website explains the
Bermuda Triangle and includes a map of the area,
theories about the disappearances there, and information about the best-known disappearances.

Team Curse (http://teamcurse.com/index.php).
This website features articles about curses that have
been placed on sports team. It includes the Curse
of the Billy Goat and the Curse of the Bambino.

Smithsonian Channel, "Stories from the Vault: The
Hope Diamond" (www.smithsonianchannel.com/
site/sn/video/player/latest-videos/stories-from-
the-vaults-the-hope-diamond/595091773001/).
This is a short video about the journey of the
Hope Diamond and how it eventually ended up at
the Smithsonian.

Index

Picture Credits

About the Author

Rachel Lynette has written over 70 books for children of all ages as well as creative and critical-thinking resource materials for teachers. She lives in the Seattle, Washington, area with her two children, David and Lucy, and a cat named Cosette. When not writing, Lynette enjoys spending time with her family and friends, traveling, reading, drawing, crocheting colorful hats, biking, and in-line skating.